F.A.I.L. Faithfully Allowing IT Leverage

F.A.I.L.   Faithfully Allowing IT Leverage

This book was Edited, Proofed and Formatted by SPAN
(Self Published Authors Network)
Graphic Design and Book Cover by ButterflyGrapix

F.A.I.L. Faithfully Allowing IT Leverage

Copyright Page

Copyright ⓒ 2016 by Drs. Anthony and Kim Ladson

Printed in USA

ISBN 978-0-9976900-0-2

All rights reserved, No part of this publication may be reproduced, distributed, or transmitted in any form or by any means, including photocopying, recording, or other mechanical methods, without the prior written permission of the publisher, except in the case of brief quotations embodied in critical reviews and certain other noncommercial uses permitted by copyright law. For permission requests, write to the publisher at the address below.

Ordering information

Copyright 2016 The Ladson Group L.L.C.

Dratladson@gmail.com or **Kimladson@aol.com**
Ordering information;
Individual Sales go to Www.livebydesignthebook.com
Quantity Sales. Special discounts are available in quantity purchases by corporations, associations, networking groups. For details contact us at the address above or call 212-335-0943 or 212-498-9271

Www.livebydesignthebook.com

F.A.I.L. Faithfully Allowing IT Leverage

Dedication

We want to dedicate this book to every person that feels like they are stuck in an IT, a business that is not producing and yes those that feel they are stuck in a dead-end job. We dedicate this book to you because your heart is our heart. You know that you have potential that is far beyond what you currently are displaying. You know that you are not living up to that potential and IT is something you need to focus on. This book is dedicated to People who want to win and are willing to FAIL to do so.

To Our Mentor Les Brown and the Platinum Speaker Family your contribution in our life has stretched us beyond our comfort zone into a place we could have not gotten to on our own. That place is one of the IT's that have helped us to **FAIL** to win

To Dr. Edward Womack for introducing us to the SPAN BOSS Johnny "MACKnificent" Mack. The association and collaboration with you two brothers took this project further, faster and we are truly blessed because of it.

Drs. Anthony & Kim Ladson

F.A.I.L. Faithfully Allowing IT Leverage

Foreword: Johnny "MACKnificent" Mack

Is often said that failure is not an option. But to FAIL is. To fail doesn't mean to lose, or to be counted out for eternity. To fail as Dr. Anthony Ladson so eloquently explains it means...

Faithfully Allowing IT Leverage.

The key question is what exactly is **IT**. IT, is the combination of factors that impact every life. IT, is different for everyone, for you IT may be the challenge of gender or race or economic circumstances. For others IT may be the challenge of class, education or religion. But for all of us IT is what determines our lot in life.

Many of us are disappointed with what we have as a life reality. Many of us wish for something different, hope for something better, desire something altogether different. But wishing and hoping and desiring are not the elements necessary to create that life.

F.A.I.L.   Faithfully Allowing IT Leverage

When all is broken down, and all is understood, the bottom line will be **Faith**. This book FAIL, by Doctors Anthony and Kim Ladson with selected other authors, is an awesome example of overcoming IT. Our lot in life is to overcome the IT's that we face. For many people IT will destroy them, for others IT will develop them to reach greater heights and achieve more than they ever thought possible.

As we experience the IT's of our lives, it is important that we see that the IT that others face may be quite different than the IT we face. One of the cruelties of life is that those that face their IT's will point fingers at others IT's and wonder why IT is challenging them. Every IT to the person facing IT is huge. Every IT that we see others face seems inconsequential or non-monumental, but the reality is IT is both.

As I read these stories of courage and overcoming and thriving and losing and gaining, I was struck

F.A.I.L. Faithfully Allowing IT Leverage

with an odd excitement. I felt the energy necessary and needed to overcome the circumstances they faced. I understood every IT and realized that although my IT was different, IT was an IT nonetheless.

Are you facing an IT today? Have you faced an IT before? When you are challenged with your own IT, will you have a fit, or will you overcome IT? As you read each one of these incredible chapters realize that your IT is no different than anyone else's. The only difference is that you are now going through and being challenged by IT. If you employ the F.A.I.L. formula, you can fail forward and into a future devoid of IT. As each one of these authors share how they dealt with IT, look at your own IT and gain clarity and courage to overcome **IT** Faithfully.

Johnny "MACKnificent" Mack

F.A.I.L. Faithfully Allowing IT Leverage

Table of contents

Foreword: Johnny "MACKnificent" Mack v
Pay Attention Every Heartbeat Counts. 2
    By Dr. Anthony Ladson 2
About the Author: Dr. Anthony Ladson 26
Use your past as fuel for winning in life. 28
    By Johnny Martinsson 28
Bio of Johnny Martinsson 69
Your past is not your future. 72
    By Dr. Kim Ladson. 72
Bio Of Dr. Kim Ladson 101
Why Weight to Win 104
    By Lonnie Ford. 104
Bio of Lonnie Ford. 120
Learn to enjoy life's Golden Moments. 122
    By Adrian Starks 122
Bio of Adrian Starks 141

F.A.I.L.   Faithfully Allowing IT Leverage

Live by *Design*
Not by Default

F.A.I.L.   Faithfully Allowing IT Leverage

Live by *Design!* Not by Default

Pay Attention Every Heartbeat Counts.
By Dr. Anthony Ladson

The greatest advice I got in life was to pay attention. Paying attention is probably more important than any activity that you can engage in. When you pay attention everything is a teacher you are able to learn from all circumstances. Everything happens by design unless we let it happen by default. Life lived by design is a blueprint for blessings, life lived by default is a feature for failure.

We're all dealt a hand of cards, what we do with those cards determines the extent and expanse of our lives. Many people when they received the hand dealt are disappointed, depressed, disgusted and downright done. I learned to look at life and the hand I was dealt with a different set of eyes. I've learned that you don't have to receive those cards that you are dealt. You can either look at

F.A.I.L.   Faithfully Allowing IT Leverage

those cards and play them to the best of your ability or you can demand a new hand.

Let's discuss the aspect of demanding a new hand. Many times the hand we're dealt isn't as bad as we think it is. Part of the process is learning how to play the hand you were dealt. More importantly it's learning how to play the cards in any game however they are dealt, and making them appear that much better. Too many times when we receive the new hand that we demand we find that the first hand wasn't so bad after all. In life we can look at the circumstances and situations and feel that we were dealt a bad hand.

When in reality the hand wasn't as bad as we may have thought. Due to the hand we are dealt, we may act out because we can, we may not act as well as we could, we just may not act at all. We may have been dealt a hand of a specific color, gender, class, or family DNA. How we deal with

F.A.I.L. Faithfully Allowing IT Leverage

the gift we are dealt determines the quality of our life.

The ultimate responsibility of every person who has been dealt a hand in life is to believe. We all have the power of choice, we can choose to accept that hand or to reject it, you don't have to keep what you don't want.

If the cards we are dealt are bad looking, we can say these are not for me and cast them aside for a new set. Many people who've grown up in dire and desperate situations have chosen to change their situation instead of accepting that as their lot in life. They choose to change and to let education and hard work and vision change their circumstance so that it benefited them.

No one has to be a loser and no one loses unless they accept loss as their lot in life. What you see, what you project in the vision of your mind, is what becomes your reality. Poor mentality doesn't have to really become your reality. What you see becomes your reality. I was 11 years old before I realized that there was a subway under the city of New York.

I'd grown up in a rosy suburb with the new shiny red bike and an allowance and wonderful friends and schools. I could not believe that there was a subway system that ran all underneath the giant city of New York. Once I found that out, I was so excited I wanted to ride, but my dad who I was living with at the time said "no way" trying to protect me. I want to share how I came from the suburbs to the urban jungle and learned to survive and to thrive.

I met my father when I was 11. Having grown up in the suburbs of Queens, Laurelton. I didn't realize how good I had it. I began acting up and doing foolish and stupid things as a child, and my mother decided to send me to stay with my dad. I'd never

F.A.I.L.   Faithfully Allowing IT Leverage

met him and I saw this big giant hunk of a man 6 foot 2" 250 pounds, the same big bone structure as me, I was immediately intimidated and excited.

A fact is a fact, but the truth cannot be denied. You know we live looking at facts that may not be true, feelings that may not be real and faith that only has value if acted upon. I was in a brand-new world and it was time for me to start paying attention. Images often have double meanings, a lot of times what we accept for one thing may have other negative or positive connotations that we are unaware of.

Our lack of understanding or unawareness doesn't change the fact that there are other meanings to what we have ascribed our meanings to. Life is how we perceive it to be, not necessarily what it is. Our perception becomes our reality. Most of us just blindly accept what is represented, the church we attend, the teachers lessons or the pastor's sermons, we accept all that as true or fact.

Trust is something that we give freely until we get to the point of understanding, at which point, trust must be earned. Just because you are given an idea or position doesn't mean that you have to accept it, which goes back to the cards I spoke of earlier, if you feel the information is bad or the cards aren't in your favor you can request a new hand. **The power to define is the power to fulfill**. We were able to define everything that we confront, deal with, and see in life. That definition gives us the power to fulfill and create that reality.

Buses have schedules, so too do the dreams and plans and manifestation we wish to see come about in our lives. I remember for the first time catching the bus in the city. It was a daunting experience as I waited for the bus to come. I waited at the bus stop with many people. I didn't realize that there

F.A.I.L. Faithfully Allowing IT Leverage

was a prescribed time for the bus to arrive, at a specific place.

Later on I realized there was a schedule for the buses to run. That was a lesson learned that sometimes you get to schedule situations, you get to schedule your dreams to come true, you get to schedule your plans to come about, you get to schedule your life to take place.

Those who don't schedule their life end up living off of someone else's schedule and plan.

As stated earlier I grew up in the Laurelton Queens, it was an awesome place, we had two dogs, a basement and I had an allowance just for being a kid. Then I moved to Manhattan..."Concrete City" with it was nothing but starkness and the difference was like night and day.

I grew up with bikes and a basement and now I was living with utter starkness. When I first met my dad who people called Chino, I was excited. He was a boxer and it looked like he just spit me out, we were the spitting image of each other.

From the very first day there was a love-hate relationship with him. I had been bad at school before, fighting and causing chaos every day. Mom said we got to get you back on track, you been fighting teachers, beating up students and living such a sorry life.

 She said it was best that I get some strict discipline and sent me to live with dad. The most powerful thing about going to live with my dad was that he was a disciplinarian, he was strict and he was fair.

Dad taught me some very powerful life lessons that I want to share with you now the first lesson that he taught me was:

F.A.I.L. Faithfully Allowing IT Leverage

1.*Feed your mind and feed your heart.*

I looked at him incredulously and asked "what do you mean?" Dad said you feed your mind by reading, by studying, by paying attention to everything around you so that you can learn and be prepared to face life as it comes at you, cause it will.

You feed your heart by being open to love and to receive goodness and the grace that God gives us. For such a strong man those were gentle and powerful words. As I have lived my life to the point where I am now I've lived by that creed: to feed my mind every day and grow.

To feed my heart in every way, so that I can receive all the goodness that life has to offer. This taught me especially feeding my heart, that there was good in everything, but I had to search for it.

F.A.I.L. Faithfully Allowing IT Leverage

And the best way to search for it, was to be able to pay attention and feed my mind so that I would be able to see when the goodness was available. My father said the world is hard, you need to soften it by making the right choices and decisions.

Another important lesson that my dad taught me was:

2.If you find the right woman you will know.

In life we are confronted with so many different people and personalities, it's hard to know who's good for you and who's not. That's why this cardinal principle of paying attention was so important and is so important now.

It is the nature of man to explore other people and it looked as if I would never find that right woman that my dad spoke about. Yet when I did, when I found my Kim, my life lit up and I knew that I found the right one. It was the week of prayer at

F.A.I.L. Faithfully Allowing IT Leverage

the church I was attending at the time when I heard a voice coming over the sound system. Within that voice I heard a sound that caused me to listen.

My heart responded by opening the locked chambers with the key of **LOVE** and knew I had to find out who that was on the microphone that was speaking. Our souls connected and our minds meld into one. We were able to understand each other and that's important, first to understand and then to be understood. That's a milestone that each one of us needs to reach. The connection with another person with an exchange of love that leads to happiness brings the greatest joy in life.

My father taught me many lessons one of which was:

3. *Hard work pays off.*

I was spoiled and undisciplined prior to meeting my dad. He taught me that you get nothing if you

F.A.I.L.   Faithfully Allowing IT Leverage

give nothing. Hard work, which could be smart work, is necessary to get the rewards and benefits that life has to offer. I was getting an allowance prior to coming to live with my dad. Once I got there I still expected money for potato chips, popcorn and soda pop. (Back then a dollar could get you all that plus a meat patty and some candy, with change left over)

I soon realized I had to wash dishes, clean my room and do other menial tasks in order to receive anything. I honestly thought I was being punished and he didn't love me. I now know that I was being prepared to be able to deal with life and to get the rewards that I wanted and the results that I deserved.

4.*Life ain't giving you nothing that you aren't working for.*

That has stuck with me all my life, I'm so glad that he taught me to earn what I wanted, no one owes

F.A.I.L.   Faithfully Allowing IT Leverage

me anything I haven't worked for. He also taught me one of the most important lessons anyone can learn in life:

5. *That is to tell the truth always.*

"Telling the truth will never get you in trouble" he always said. I remember one-time going to Stride Rite shoes and dad decided to buy me a pair of tennis shoes. I was so excited I walked in the Stride Rite and I saw those Nikes with the three stripes (Not the one Stripe), I was so excited I had to have them. I tried them on, they were a half-size too small. I wanted them so bad I told Dad they fit.

The next day I put my socks and my brand-new Nikes on and went to school. That half-size kept rubbing up against the back of my feet and by the end of the day my feet hurt bad. I came hobbling home and he said "What's wrong?" I told him the shoes had blistered my feet and hurt something awful.

F.A.I.L. Faithfully Allowing IT Leverage

Dad taught me a valuable lesson that day *"Never, Ever Lie."* I wanted those shoes so bad I didn't care, and by the end of the day I wanted them off my feet so bad I didn't care. After he whipped me, I cared a lot learned the valuable lesson that lie is never good.

But the most important lessons that he taught me was one that has changed my life and make my life worth living. That lesson was:

6. *Always keep a song in your heart.*

I remember when I first met him. He would be sitting in the living room playing some of the greats like Sam Cooke or Harry Belafonte. He would sing with such fervor and joy that I just loved to hear him sing. I would ask him who they were and he would tell me. I would just think he sounds so much better than the record because he was singing it with joy and made it look like he knew what the song was about, not just the words.

F.A.I.L.   Faithfully Allowing IT Leverage

When you discover the song in your heart even the difficult things will become easier to deal with. You won't have to continually look at and be disgusted and depressed by the circumstances that you face in life. Instead you can face them with a song in your heart, which leads to joy. Joy comes from the inside, happiness is just something that happens on the outside. You get to choose joy, you have to learn and earn happiness.

The last and most important lesson that he taught was that:

7. *Everything you go through is there for a reason pay attention cause you don't want to lose out on the lesson.*

So often we deal with circumstances that we are unhappy with. We find ourselves in situations that we wish were different or better. We want to just get through them, so that we can get to where we want to be. Everything happens for a reason, we may not see that reason right up front, but in the by-and-by we will discover it. Pay attention to the details, don't miss out on the moments, you may miss out on the lesson life is trying to teach you. You see life gives us clues in different messages. We may miss out on what life is trying to teach us on how to succeed if we don't pay attention.

Life is rough but you can make it if you pay attention. You can request more cards like we talked about earlier and then realize that the first set wasn't so bad after all. You can wish you had a better nose, different color, had more height, or more girth. Be careful what you wish for because you just might get it. You have to accept what you desire, because if you're asking for the desire, and you want it, once you get it you've got to accept even if it is not what you want, you have to be prepared to deal with it.

F.A.I.L. Faithfully Allowing IT Leverage

A lesson or two that life taught me is that *if you don't do the requirements, you can't expect the success results.* The results are what you receive once the requirements have been met. Let me share with you three top clues that life gives you for success.

#1: *If you like to do something that is easy for you but hard for someone else, you've discovered a blueprint for passion to cash in on success.*

Excellence creates Success

#2: *If you can enjoy doing what you do and others do too, and it aligns up with your passion... that's a clue that that may be something you can cash in on.*

What I mean by that is, something that you do that makes you feel wonderful, makes you feel good, gives you joy, and when you do, it makes other

F.A.I.L. Faithfully Allowing IT Leverage

people feel good to, that's a clue that's what you should be pursuing doing.

You know the stars and the moon are separate things. God created them different, one greater and one lesser. The sun was created to sustain life on earth, share with you brightness and cause crops to grow etc. The moon was placed so that it can regulate the waters and the tides and the different aspects of what keeps the gravitational flow in order. Both are important, both are necessary, one is not necessarily greater than the other, but they both have a purpose.

#3: If you see something that irritates you, and you can do it easier, better or Quicker....that's a clue, it may be the passion that you can cash in on.

Many times I have seen chairs in place but out of order. They may have been uneven or a mismatched number. My inclination has always

F.A.I.L. Faithfully Allowing IT Leverage

been to straighten them or set them in order. This could indicate that I have a flair for order or event planning. Always pay attention to what you pay attention to, that may be the passion that you can cash in on.

A Test I Thought I Failed

So all of this lines up for the final part that I want to share with you.. this is the test that I thought that I failed. I thought that I was paying attention and I realize now that every heartbeat counts. I came home from school and found my dad lying on the living room floor. I went to wake him. Checking in, I tried to rouse him and tried to get him up and he didn't respond, I realized that there was a problem. Several weeks earlier I'd seen the show Punky Brewster, and she had performed CPR and saved the life of her best friend Cherrie, one of the characters on the show. I realized that I had to do that procedure to save my dad's life. I began the chest compressions and the mouth breathing, and the nose holding on my dad. All seemingly to no avail.

I screamed at the top of my lungs to my mother and told her to "Call 911 Jimmy is not breathing!" I continued to do what I thought that I'd seen on television and still my dad wasn't breathing. What seemed like hours but was only minutes, the paramedics came and they did what they could and shortly thereafter came in and said "we're sorry, he is gone."

That experience devastated me. I should have been paying attention, and yet even though I had watched the program I didn't pay attention enough to save my dad.

The next two years saw me falling into despondency and depression. I could not forgive myself for not being able to revive my dad. I acted out in ways that were unacceptable to his memory. My grades fell dramatically and I was put into

F.A.I.L.   Faithfully Allowing IT Leverage

Special Ed. Constantly fighting, getting suspended and in short acting a total fool.

One day as I was sitting solemnly in my room, my sister came in and asked "What is wrong with you?"

" What do you mean?"I asked

She said "why are you so mad all the time."

I broke down and cried like a baby I told her that I blamed myself for not being able to save Jimmy after having watched that Punky Brewster show. She laughed and said "you idiot, Jimmy was alive when the paramedics arrived, they told me he was alive. They said that if you had not done what you did they would not have had any chance to be able to save him. They just weren't able to do anymore because he was just too far gone with other aspects of the heart attack. He was still alive because of what **YOU** did."

That changed my life that gave me a new perspective.

My mom came into the room as it was obvious that something was wrong. She asked about it, when my sister told her why I had been being such a jerk, she smiled and said "Tony you are blessed, your dad was there when you were born into this world and he loved you and you were there when he left this world and you loved him that should be enough."

That set me free and since that time I've been on a mission to help other people that are stuck in areas that they can control yet don't know how. I paid attention, that day, I did all I could do, what I did was enough, more than enough. When you pay attention to the circumstances of life you will find that every heartbeat counts and you can make a difference.

F.A.I.L. Faithfully Allowing IT Leverage

Epilogue: How I leveraged failure.

Life is so full of details the only way to enjoy it is to pay attention. Circumstances like threats, trials, fiery furnace situations, all come along ultimately to make us better. When you pay attention you will find the courage to go out and live your dream because you will see every little detail that makes the difference.

Don't give up on your dreams, cash in on your passion, you have the power and the courage to live your dreams then you will feel the joy of life. You should, people always used to ask me what to do in certain situations as if I was a young Dr. Phil, Dr. Laura, or a New York Oprah. I just have learned to pay attention along the way. I've learned the life lessons that my dad taught me to learn from life itself.

F.A.I.L. Faithfully Allowing IT Leverage

You have to pay attention to what you are passionate about. **Living someone else's dream is a job, living your own dreams is purpose.** Pay attention to what you desire to do, that lies in your passion. Get the greatness out and live the dream. That's what life is all about. Perception of failure becomes fulfilled in the long run with what you decide to do, that is the secret to your success have a great day!

F.A.I.L. Faithfully Allowing IT Leverage

About the Author: Dr. Anthony Ladson

Dr. Anthony T. Ladson is a John Maxwell Certified leadership Speaker/Trainer and Coach who helps executives, marketplace leaders, and senior pastors reduce the stress and frustration associated with the gap that exists between their faith in God and their corporate actions and responsibilities.

Utilizing the Platinum Leadership of EXCELLENCE Formula, a proprietary methodology designed specifically to address how Christian leaders can be high performance leaders who are capable of building and sustaining high performance teams while maintaining their ethical and moral standards, Dr. Anthony T. Ladson is able to improve leadership performance by providing solutions that are elegantly simple, yet highly effective.

Contact Dr. Ladson at: Dratladson@gmail.com

F.A.I.L. Faithfully Allowing IT Leverage

Live by *Design!* Not by Default

F.A.I.L. Faithfully Allowing IT Leverage

Use your past as fuel for winning in life.

By Johnny Martinsson

It was an early morning in April. I held my gym bag in my tiny hand as I was walking through the hallway on my way to the front door, when something suddenly happened. I froze for a second and then turned around and ran back through the house and into my room, where I crawled in under the bed. I was just seven years old, but still to this day I remember everything about that moment. How it smelled, what it looked like, the sounds, but most of all, how it felt. It was as if my body was paralyzed, my brain was working but the body was shut off.

If I close my eyes right now, I'm there. I can see the dust on the floor closest to the wall, I can hear the sound of my heart beating inside my chest, as well as my mother's footsteps coming towards my room, the smell of wood from the beds structure. I

F.A.I.L. Faithfully Allowing IT Leverage

remember it all, but most of all I remember the paralyzing feeling making me unable to move, or speak, but it wasn't actually that terrifying. The feeling as I recall it is more of not understanding what was going on, why I was doing what I was doing? That was scary.

What made this event even weirder was the fact that I was on my way to play my first ever soccer match, something I had been dreaming of for as long as I could remember. Well, being seven it wasn't that long in actuality, but in reality it was literally all I had ever dreamed of so far in my entire lifetime. And now when the day had finally come, here I was under my bed, hiding in the dark. I couldn't believe it myself but I wasn't able to break the state.

So my mother walked in, stood beside my bed and said: "Johnny, if you don't want to play today that's absolutely fine. We'll just call the coach and tell him that you will play the next game instead, okay?" And then something happened inside of me. I was on the edge, do or die time for a seven year old "soccerprowannabe", and I guess I realized I had to make a decision: Take a chance and maybe win, take no chance and definitely lose. Unfortunately, I can't recall that moment of making my decision or what thought process took place, but it doesn't really matter. The result was the important factor and I did beat the ugly fears and left them there under the bed as I crawled back out and marched out to the car. And off to the game we went.

Today I'm a big man, standing 6ft-"4" above ground, but at age seven I was not big. I was as short and scrawny as any other kid on that team. And the game was held at a huge soccer field, I remember it looking like a big ocean when I stepped out on it. But the initial fear was not there anymore as the referee blew his whistle.

F.A.I.L. Faithfully Allowing IT Leverage

I honestly don't remember anything from playing the game, how I did or if we won. But I do remember what happened during the intermission. The first period of the game was done and we were standing in the middle of the huge field drinking water out of little plastic cups. I didn't know any of the other guys, maybe one or two from school, but I guess that was part of my initial fear, being alone. But as we stood there, I heard a loud voice yelling out, "who in our team is wearing number seven today?"

It was a burly kid called Oscar who I was a little scared of actually, he was also a year older than me. And as I looked down my jersey realizing I was number seven … My heart started pounding real hard. And Oscar didn't stop, he kept yelling so I raised my hand and said with a mouse like voice: "That's me." He turned around, fixed me with his eyes and set off towards me. He stopped right in front of me, looked me up and down and said:

F.A.I.L.   Faithfully Allowing IT Leverage

"What's your name?" My mouth was as dry as the dust on the soccer field when I answered: "Johnny. My name is Johnny." Oscar stared at me, I didn't know what to expect when he suddenly patted me on the shoulder and said: "Okay Johnny, damn you're good!" He grinned at me and turned around and walked away. And I walked into a life that was totally focused on soccer for my entire youth. Actually, I still play soccer, 39 years later. But that's another story.

Using earlier successes in your present life challenges.

This event that I just shared with you happened to me as a very young boy. Many times I have wondered what my life would have looked like if I had given in and let the fear of failure beat me down and kept me under my bed. Because I wasn't one of the tough kids when I grew up. I had a great home and a family that loved me, and I've always had friends. But inside I wasn't tough at all.

F.A.I.L. Faithfully Allowing IT Leverage

Afraid of the dark which made me sleep with the lights turned on for most of my childhood. But defeating the fears that day and playing that soccer game, receiving the confirmation of my capacity as a soccer player, rocket launched me in terms of believing in myself and my abilities. It also made me more self confident and I could start turning off the lights at night. Something had shifted inside of me. Because I dared.

About a year after being adopted in to the world of soccer, I wanted to venture out into the game of hockey. Because back in those days, soccer was more of a spring-summer sport, and I wanted something to do during the winters as well. So I went with my next door neighbor to the hockey practice, and actually I wasn't good. At all. Running with a ball is one thing, skating on an ice rink handling a stick and a puck at the same time, a little bit trickier. But what happened then probably wouldn't happen today, though.

F.A.I.L.   Faithfully Allowing IT Leverage

After the second practice I participated in, I was asked by the coach to stay after practice along with one other boy. So when the other boys went to the locker room, he turned to us and said: "Well guys, it's like this. You are of course welcome for practice, but you won't be playing any games, okay? You are simply too bad and it won't work. But if you want to come for practice, I won't stop you." I was eight years old.

Now, I don't know how I would have reacted without the soccer story in my backpack. But I do actually remember not being sad, it actually made sense to me, I knew I was horrible on the skates. But I didn't break down, I didn't cry. I went home to practice. I was not good enough then, but I knew I could be if I just learned how to skate and handle the stick.

I don't know how many hours my father helped me develop my soccer skills on the backyard growing up, throwing balls at me to practice headers or just handling the ball in speed. When I came home with my declaration that I needed to practice my skating, he organized, along with another couple of fathers, so that they could get water supply and fill up the old soccer field in our neighborhood and turning it in to a ice rink during the winters. And there I was, from straight after school until mother called me in and it was so dark I couldn't even see any more.

When the next season started, my father drove me to hockey practice. We stood outside and listened to the roaring from the locker room as it was filled with boys with energy. I didn't know anyone in there, but I didn't care. In my heart I knew I was ready. Not to prove anything to the coach, no feelings of revenge, I just wanted to play. My father looked at me as he heard the shouting from inside the locker room, and he said with a hesitating, mild voice: "Son, are you sure you want to do this? I mean, you don't have to, you know that, right?"

I just kept looking at the locker room door and said: "I know dad. I just want to." And then I opened the door and stepped right in to the bunch of screaming animals who after that day became my friends and teammates. With no fear or doubt in my mind. I remember that day as strongly as I do my time under the bed.

Being on a sports field, whether it be a soccer field or an ice rink, did something to me. And still does today. Stepping on to that surface, crossing the line from ordinary life in to the sports world, is for me a little bit like when Clark Kent goes in to the phone booth and comes out as Superman. It may look like the same person, in tights though, but the mindset is different. The self-image is different. The beliefs are different. And knowing that it's possible to achieve seemingly unachievable things if you just work hard, can really move mountains.

F.A.I.L. Faithfully Allowing IT Leverage

And if you are contained by a lot of rules in life as how or what you should or should not be or do, then sports can be a big break from that burden.

Have you ever wondered why so many sport stars have it so hard ending their career? The number of comebacks for professional boxers is ridiculous. Why? Because that's the only place where they feel that they fit in, where they are in control and where their otherwise fragile self-image is the one of a Champion. Not easy to walk away from, trust me.

When I stepped across the white sidelines of the soccer field, I changed. When I skated on to the ice surface, I changed. But back then, I wasn't aware, I just followed my instincts. Nothing wrong with that sometimes, but if we want to learn how to use our strengths and draw from our past experiences, we have to become aware. No one could demand that from a child of course, then life is about growing, learning and making mistakes. Following feelings and instincts. It is then we lay the foundation for a life we design based on what we've learned so far, instead of a life determined by how someone else may want or think is right for you. Awareness. Taking control, moving over from the passenger seat to the driver seat. Two hands on the wheel, right foot on the gas pedal. And also ready to hit the brakes when needed. Can you feel it?

For me, the road of Life ended in a dark hole, still with the foot on the gas, when I was just 19 years old. I still to this day remember every feeling, every sound and sight of that moment. And as that happened, I didn't have any exit strategy.

One of the biggest reasons I wanted to ever start playing soccer was because I had a clear vision of Why. And my Why was because I wanted to play for IFK Gothenburg, the best team in Sweden. My entire family went to see their home games and every fiber of my little body wanted to walk out on the arena dressed in that blue and white uniform, one day.

And without understanding the concept at that young age, I started visualizing myself running out and receiving the standing ovation from the crowd. I saw my parents and other relatives happy faces in the stands and I felt the rush in my body. Every night as I lay in my bed, before I went to sleep, I lived in that dream. I saw myself running and scoring, how I ran down the field and how my team mates caught up with me and threw themselves at me. That was what I took with me in my dreams from the age of seven.

When I was 15 years old I received a phone call. "Hello, my name is Tony and I'm the coach for IFK Gothenburg, the youth academy. We have been following you and we would love for you to come and play for us. Are you interested?" I remember saying yes and writing down the address and time for the first practice, but that's about it.

F.A.I.L.   Faithfully Allowing IT Leverage

Oh, and then I screamed. Loud and with all of my lungs capacity.

Nine years of practicing every day, more than often twice a day, a lot of pain but never complaining. Pushing myself beyond every limit all the time. And as I understood much later, putting myself there emotionally every night visualizing. It wasn't luck, and I wasn't the biggest talent, far from it. But I was dedicated, and my vision was crystal clear. And that call was the pay off. I had reached my goal.

I lived my dream for two years, playing for the team in my heart. It was everything I had ever imagined. Rain, snow or sunshine, it didn't matter, we played almost every day but I don't have any memories of ever not wanting to go. And I played well, especially the first year. I got to travel a lot, make new friends and make the most of my talent as an athlete. Life was brilliant.

F.A.I.L. Faithfully Allowing IT Leverage

After the second season we had to wait for an extension of our contracts. I was promised I would have my place for the next season so I wasn't that nervous. But as the day for signing came closer I started to doubt myself. The second season was for a big portion spoiled by injuries for me, but I finished strong. Something just felt a little off … And then the phone rang.

I heard the words on the phone as my coach told me that he was really sad to let me know that those higher up had decided to go in a different direction. Despite the fact that we won the first League with ten points and were undefeated for the season, we were not given an extension. We all had to go. I said good bye and just sat there staring at the wall. It was like I had been watching a movie and now the screen went blank. I had failed. An epic fail. I was given the opportunity of a lifetime and I blew it.

F.A.I.L. Faithfully Allowing IT Leverage

I had a lot of offers from other clubs, so continuing my soccer career wasn't a problem. The problem was that I had lost my vision. My Why. I did sign for another team and I did play for them the next season. But without any heart or passion. In my mind it was a huge step backwards and didn't at all relate to what I used to envision. So during a game, in which I was substituted, I had made up my mind: I was done with soccer. So I turned in my uniform and left. Feeling like a complete failure.

What happened after that was like a string of bad choices. I didn't practice anything for almost a year. I didn't move more than necessary, ate bad food and was miserable. One day I sat at home and thought about where I was in life. I worked at a job I hated, I was in a relationship that was going nowhere … And most of all, I had no dream, no vision. I didn't know where to go, feeling completely lost.

F.A.I.L.   Faithfully Allowing IT Leverage

So I went in to a depression. And then my body just collapsed. I started to feel sick and my body was in massive pain. I was taken to the hospital several times for what turned out to be panic attacks when I thought I was having a heart attack. But sick I was, so I was hospitalized for over a month. I was 20 years old and had gone from Superman to a rusty bucket of nothing in one year. And I was told I probably would be in a wheelchair because of a surgery they wanted to perform on my back. And I thought I was going to die.

But I didn't. I refused the operation. I remember the Doctor telling me I had one medical choice to maybe get my disease in remission. And scared as I was of the side effects, I took it. I remember standing in the city by the canal, thinking about jumping. But I also recall the feeling growing inside, telling me "you can beat this! You have won before and you can do it again! It's possible!"

F.A.I.L.   Faithfully Allowing IT Leverage

And I realized how much I loved life, that I had always loved life with all its opportunities and adventures. I wasn't done yet, far from it! In my head I went back to the little boy under the bed that broke free and dared to step out and face what needed to be faced. If I could do it when I was seven, I was damn sure I could make it now.

And I did. Less than a year later I was back on track, playing soccer and got myself a new job. I also had the great blessing of becoming a father to a beautiful boy, my son Nathanael. As I look at him today when he's become a strong and beautiful man, I feel incredibly grateful for finding that inner strength and a method to fight my way back. Yes, I think of it as a method. When you find something to return to when extra strength is needed, you have a method. I have a method now that I can use to help others, and that is something I thank those days wandering in darkness for.

F.A.I.L.   Faithfully Allowing IT Leverage

Section 2: Your feelings are the messengers from your soul.

Sometimes life takes you out on a road trip. One that you hadn't planned and absolutely didn't want to take, but it's not your decision. You just have to pick up and leave without even having time to pack your things, not even a toothbrush or clean underwear. At the time you may curse and cry, scream at the heavens and beg for mercy, or maybe you decide to curl up in your bed all alone and shut the world out.

It's different for everybody how we deal with hard times and if you have been there, you know what your strategies are. And as **Les Brown** once said when I attended one of his seminars, about going through a dark time in life*:* *"Well, either you've been there and recently come out of it, or if not, you're going to get there soon. Isn't life beautiful, right?"* And of course he laughed Les Brown style.

F.A.I.L. Faithfully Allowing IT Leverage

But he's right. No one gets through life without being forced by certain events to go deep within themselves. It's called crisis, but I would prefer renaming it connecting. Connecting with your true self, your soul, your deepest source of information and infinite possibilities. If these moments in our lives didn't occur, we would never do it.

We would never go after that source of information about ourselves and why we are here. Why? Because it's hard! It's hard, it's a long winding uphill climb, and we don't really know what kind of reward there is when we reach the top. And no one can tell you because we all have different peaks to reach when we're climbing the mountain of getting to know who we really are, what we're capable of.

"Who am I?" The question of all questions, that everyone will ask themselves probably more than one or two times during a lifetime. Why am I really here, what am I really good at, will I ever

succeed in anything in life, why does all of this have to happen to me ... Questions that are directed towards a higher source, but actually should be aimed inwards rather than outside ourselves.

Whether you believe in God or not, that shouldn't pose a problem. Because if you don't believe in God then you should at least believe in yourself and that you have the power to change your life. And if you do believe in God, then you probably believe that you are created by God and your soul is connected to the Spirit.

For me, my journey really started shortly before reaching the age of thirty. I felt like I had gone 15 rounds against a hungry and fit Mike Tyson, beaten and bruised, down on hands and knees. I didn't realize then that Life was pushing me towards my individual starting point for destination *"Me."* So I did what most of us do: resisted. Refused to listen or see the signs that popped up along the way until I ended up missing a corner and crashed in to a wall. The wall of *"time to wake up and start climbing."* I felt scared, lost and really small. I didn't see any way out of where I had put myself, or who to ask for directions. But, as it usually happens: help came in a way I never would have expected.

One day my mother called me and asked me to come with her on a meeting. She told me about this man who others said had the ability to see what you need to know in your life, especially if you had turned the wrong corner and had no GPS. I was really skeptical, but I figured I had nothing to lose so I came along for the ride. Still skeptical though.

I entered a small room in a little cottage on the countryside. It smelled like an old vacation home that hadn't been used since last summer and needed a real change of air. For a second I felt like just turning around and run out of there, like that little boy I once was. Then a knock on the door, and he entered. He greeted me with a big smile and I could feel his warmth as he shook my hand. "Are you sure we haven't met before? You feel really familiar", he said. "I don't think we have sir", I replied. He smiled and told me to relax and just let whatever messages that I needed the most come through. And so we began.

I won't transcribe the entire conversation. But that hour changed the direction of my life. Afterwards I cried for days, but not tears of sadness. Okay, a little bit but only because we talked about things very close to my heart, but maybe mostly because I realized how I had squandered so many of the gifts I had been given. How I had been focusing on everything I didn't have or failed at, instead of all I actually had in my life. And the possibilities that lie ahead of me, but I refused to see. My perception was way off, so to speak. I was stuck in my past and what went wrong then and those

F.A.I.L. Faithfully Allowing IT Leverage

feelings had me imprisoned. It was a moment of true clarity. An eye-opener if you will.

He said a couple of things I do want to share. Because I think they can also be useful for you. For me they where life changing. Maybe they can bring something positive in to your life as well.

The first thing he said was this: *"You look at yourself as a failure. A looser. Let me tell you my friend, you are not! What you are, is lost. You were going somewhere, that road wasn't right and you ended up driving around looking for the right exit. And when the sign came up you didn't see it, because you were still looking for the old sign. So you have just kept on driving, without any meaning or goal, just feeling empty and lost. And that is a terribly destructive way to live your life, right?"*

He looked at me with his big eyes steadily focused on mine. Tears were running down my face, because that insight was so true that I felt the pain all the way to the core. "Yes, you're right. Can you help me find the way out of here", I asked? He

F.A.I.L. Faithfully Allowing IT Leverage

leaned forward in his chair, put his hands together under the chin before he answered.

"It's actually quite simple my friend. Here's what you're going to do: Listen to your feelings, put words to them and then act upon them. Your feelings are the messengers from your soul, and they will never tell you a lie."

I took that to heart. Along with some other things that I needed to hear. I realized I had stopped growing, become complacent. So I went back to the University and finished my exam. But what I had realized most of all, I needed to work on myself. I was a father myself now and if nothing else I had to grow up, take responsibility for my life, who I was and what kind of person I wanted my children, and the world, to see.

Shortly after meeting the man with the truth I started seeing a therapist. But after our second meeting I realized it didn't do anything for me. I could hear his voice in my head saying *"listen to your feelings, they are the messengers from your soul,"* and I did listen. I got up from the chair and paid my bill and told her that I wouldn't come back. Not that she had done anything wrong, it just wasn't for me.

As the door to her office closed behind me I started walking down the street. It wasn't my intention but I felt drawn in to the bookstore right across the street and without any further hesitation I went in. Immediately I just walked up to one of the shelves and pulled out a book. It was colorless, grey actually and I just knew it was the one I wanted. As I read the cover it said: "Your subconscious power central", and was written by a German hypnotherapist. I bought the book and went home, read it from cover to cover.

As I read it, I remembered a few years earlier having read another book that had impacted me a lot, actually at the moment it felt like something really hit home for me. It was called "Many lives, Many masters", written by Dr. Brian L. Weiss. It was a spellbinding case history about him using

F.A.I.L. Faithfully Allowing IT Leverage

hypnotherapy to treat a young girl with clinical depression. In fact, that book is probably still today the one book that has impacted me the most. The one I picked up at the bookstore was just a reminder of where I was supposed to go. Because as life had gone downhill I had forgotten about the book and now it all came back to me as an avalanche.

I picked up the Yellow pages, (yes, this was before internet), and started looking for a therapist that practiced hypnotherapy. I found three. So I called all of them and left a message on their machines. One called back and told me that he was fully booked so it was no chance there. Actually one of them never ever even returned my phone call. But the third one did. And as great things happen when we follow our feelings, he took me on. And that was when everything started.

It is hard to describe how much meeting Dr. Robert S. Jerden has meant to me. Having that

F.A.I.L.   Faithfully Allowing IT Leverage

epiphany at the bookstore that sent me on to the road that inside I knew was the right one for me, opened up a whole new meaning in my life. I found not only myself, but also my Purpose. My Why. And isn't that what we're all looking for, the reason for us being on this planet?

Since you are reading this book I know that you are one of those people who has asked that question more than once, am I right? I know I've asked myself that question more times than is countable. But now I know, and with that comes a great certainty, to know what direction to aim for. It does not mean that everything you go for from that point is absolutely right, but you know what to look for. And if you should find yourself missing the target, you will know what adjustment you need to do to get the arrow to hit the target next time. And that is a huge difference.

I started out as Robert S. Jerden's patient. The effects from the hypnosis was staggering and after about six months, when we said goodbye as I was "healed", I drove my car to my favorite place in my hometown: The Botanical Gardens. I don't know how many hours I've spent there, lost in confusion and despair, among the beautiful trees and flowers. But that day, something was totally different. I remember as I passed through the gates and entered the park, I was certain that I was walking a couple of inches above the ground.

I felt light as air and I remember looking over my shoulder to see if anyone was staring at me as I was floating above the surface, but I was all alone. I followed the small road up the garden, passed the green hills and trees and the pond with all the goldfishes on my way up to my special spot. There is a space in the garden called the Japanese valley and there was a bench where I used to sit and think about life. And somehow I needed to proof test this wonderful feeling I had, to see if I really felt this good, if it was possible.

F.A.I.L. Faithfully Allowing IT Leverage

I sat down on the bench and I actually tried to think of something really bad. I tried to bring up something trying and difficult to the surface and tried hard. But there was nothing! After giving it my best I finally surrendered to the feelings of joy and happiness. Bliss, almost. I cried, but good tears.

What did we do, you probably wonder? Well, first we started with behavioral modification through hypnosis. Changing the codes in my hard drive, my subconscious. And after that we took on the hard work of cleansing me of painful memories that got stuck inside my system using hypnosis to get in touch with them, since most of us suppress those memories to enable us to live on and move on. They become just like a slow, low key inflammation inside of us. Sometimes they show up in different forms but we don't really know what's ailing.

Just an annoying itch inside. Anyway, we cleared it all. I won't lie, it was hard. Painful at times and

F.A.I.L. Faithfully Allowing IT Leverage

really exhausting, but in the end, totally worth it. That was the reason for me feeling like floating after that final visit. I was light. My baggage had been dropped.

My relationship with Dr. Jerden didn't end there. Of course. Actually I knew after the first time we spoke over the phone that this man was going to be very significant in my life. And I was right. You see, after we were done being doctor/ patient, it didn't take long before our relationship took on another form.

"You have a gift for this Johnny, and I want to train you, mentor you, to help you become all that I know you can be. If you want to, I will offer my fullest support and teach you everything I possibly can to help you reach your true potential. If you say yes I have a room here at my clinic for you. I will help you through the trainings required and be your supervisor to ensure your grades. I will even

F.A.I.L. Faithfully Allowing IT Leverage

provide patients for you as you get started in the business. How does that sound to you?"

Robert S. Jerden looked at me, and I guess I looked funny with my jaw hanging down. I tried to take in what he just offered me, what seemed to be a Golden ticket in to the world I wanted to enter. The problem was just that I was lost for words, he realized that and smiled. "Should I take that as a yes", he said. I nodded my head. "Great, let's get started!" he shouted and jumped out of his chair.

That was 17 years ago. And he kept his word on every account. All the way until he sadly passed away much too early two years ago, he was my friend, my mentor, my teacher. And as he kept pointing out, my colleague. There was no end to his generosity towards me and my growing as a hypnotherapist, nothing he didn't want me to take part of or take in. It was like he knew his time was ticking and he didn't want to let everything he'd learned through his 35 years practicing clinical hypnotherapy to go to waste. I was somehow being part of his legacy, and I feel more honored as time goes and the more I take that in. Gifts come in different ways, and what a gift I was given.

But a gift is one thing. It's what you do with it that will really make a difference. Of course, you can just sit back and be comfortable with what you have. But when you take that gift and put yourself and your unique talents together, that's when magic happens! The difference between mediocrity and excellence. If you have the willingness to reach your true potential, you have to strive for excellence. And that is only possible thru hard work and adding you in to the mix. You have something special, something unique, and that's what you have to give to the world. Then nothing can stop you on your way to living your true potential.

So I did. I kept studying, went to courses and seminars, as I still do. Because no one is ever at

F.A.I.L. Faithfully Allowing IT Leverage

the final destination and if you start to think that, you are on the wrong track! Not only will you keep adding value to your clients by knowing more and having more tools and ways to help them, I have never been at a seminar or education without making at least one new great connection.

As a matter of fact it's because I went on a plane from Sweden to New York to attend a seminar with Les Brown that I'm having the wonderful opportunity to be a part of this book. Because of the connections I made there. And in addition to that I learned great things that I use all the time and made some really great friends that enriched my life. The law of Universe decrees, *everything most grow or it will die.* And when we stop growing, we start losing interest and life becomes less interesting. Don't let that happen to you.

If you stop people on the street and ask them if they are living life by their own design or just following another's blueprint, what would be their answer? Well, if you put the question like that they may think you're gone crazy. But if they get the message most people will answer that "of course I think for myself."

We all know that's not true. Most people are followers and actually don't want to think for themselves. They live their lives on autopilot and if they crash it's not their fault, it's the system. Or at least someone within the system. We live in a society of unawareness. We just do what we do, working to pay the bills and have enough to get by until we wither up and die. It may sound harsh and sad, but it's true. How many people do you know that have sat down and looked at their lives, finding out what they really want to do and then put together a plan of action to make it in to reality? Can you even think of anyone?

Because of the success stories we read about some people, we know that it is possible. But the majority believe it's not for them. That those who

F.A.I.L. Faithfully Allowing IT Leverage

made it to their dream destination are cut from another cloth, that they have something others don't. People often ask me why it's so difficult to change.

The number one reason as I see it after working on myself, and with other people, for more than 20 years is because: **A)** It's hard. It takes really hard work, determination and perseverance to change the course just a little bit. Even though that little bit probably will make all the difference. **B)** It takes time for the new ways of being and acting to be reprogrammed in our system. After all, until you start the process of reprogramming, you have followed the old blueprint and which you now have to override.

Working with people, that is the conclusion I always come back to. You have to be patient and be willing to keep going, even when there's no notable difference on the outside. When you go to the gym you don't expect to see your body

F.A.I.L. Faithfully Allowing IT Leverage

transform after a week. But when it comes to changing our behavior we just want to go and get a pill and be done with it.

If you want to take your life down a new, healthier, happier path, you will have to work for it! There is no way around it, over it or under it. You have to work right through it and past it. No other way is possible! And that is not what most people want to hear. In our modern society we have eliminated the "space between." We are used to want something and get immediate satisfaction of our needs. When we call someone on the cellphone and they don't answer, or call back in an instant, we get annoyed. Irritated.

We don't have any patience at all, we are often frustrated and stressed out, unsatisfied. If you are old enough to remember how it was before we all carried around our phones in our pocket, you also remember that several times during the day we

F.A.I.L. Faithfully Allowing IT Leverage

disconnected. When we sat down on the bus or the subway, we disconnected.

After a while our minds drifted as we stared out the window and our brains actually shifted from fully alert –Beta mode, to Alpha state, which is the same as going into light hypnosis. You can actually measure the brainwaves and see the change between the states take place. Our entire system then immediately started to repair and recharge.

When we take the same ride today, what happens? Everybody on that bus has their Smartphone up and eyes fixed on the screen. If someone isn't doing that, he probably had it stolen. We can forget almost anything when we leave for work except for the phone, that's a disaster. Not only do we miss all the pleasant conversation and new meetings that can occur in a situation like that, but the worst thing is that we never disconnect. Our brains are on full alert all the time. Beta-mode all the way. And that goes on all the way until we go to bed at night, with watching television and being online until we brush our teeth.

Actually after that we check the phone once more before we put it down beside the bed … And then we think it's strange that we can't fall asleep. Or that we wake up in the middle of the night, not able to get a good night's sleep other than when we are totally exhausted. Or have been to the doctor and got a prescription of sleeping pills to knock us out.

That constant being in Beta-mode causes us to burn out. It builds up stress that eventually shows up physically in the way of different symptoms as pain, usually headache or in the stomach, dizziness, anxiety, you name it.

And then we go to the doctor. Because we don't want to see the real cause of our condition because that will mean we have to change something. And

F.A.I.L. Faithfully Allowing IT Leverage

that will take work and since we're already tired and stressed out we don't want to add, what we perceive it as, more work. No we want the pill so we can get back to our lives and continue as we were.

But when the body starts signaling, it won't back down. It will start with a light knock on your door. If you don't listen it will knock a little harder. If you still decide to ignore it, it will eventually bang so hard that it will break down your entire door to get your attention. By that time, nothing else will probably mean anything in comparison to what it has to say. Nothing else will be distracting and the message will be in neon across your wall as you sit there staring at it, wondering why you didn't see that coming at all.

Even though change is hard and takes time, there are ways to speed it up. And that is why I initially got into hypnosis. Because it goes directly in to your hard wire, your subconscious mind where all the collected data lies. And it also goes around the ever doubting, analyzing and therefore hindering conscious mind.

If you compare it to ordinary therapy where you go and talk to someone for years, you have to deal with all the mental faculties and defense barriers that we have set up to protect ourselves with. They are there to help us, of course, but when you try to impress new ideas, new behaviors that goes against what you have been programmed to believe, it will work against you. That is why it takes such a long time for you to accept it and welcome the change. With hypnosis you don't have to deal with that resistance to change and therefore you can move so much faster along the new road of being. And since you have already established what doesn't work and what changes are needed together with your hypnotherapist, you don't have any use for that resistance that is active on the conscious level, right?

F.A.I.L.   Faithfully Allowing IT Leverage

But even if using hypnosis is a faster way to elicit change, like everything else it's not for everyone. There will never be "One way" to achieve the life we want, because we are all different. And that is wonderful! How boring wouldn't it had been if everyone functioned in the exact same way? So for some people the process of change will feel better in a slower pace, as in long-time therapy. And that's fine. Or something completely different in the wide range of ways to become the real You. The only thing that matters is that you find your way, someone and something that resonates inside, that feels real, and that you move along that path. That's what is going to make the difference. That you move. Remember, nothing moves until You do. So find your way and just go!

Bio of Johnny Martinsson

Born April 14th 1970 in Gothenburg, Sweden, Johnny Martinsson is already an established author in his home country. He has two books published in Sweden and they are both novels but they are built on a strong psychological theme. The goal has always been to enter the American market of books, and especially in the field of improving the quality of people's lives.

Growing up there was only one thing on his mind: being a professional soccer player, the number one sport in Sweden. When that plan fell through, he went back to University and finished with a Bachelor degree in Sociology. But that was only the start and he went on to become a Clinical Hypnotherapist, Licensed Life Coach, NLP Practitioner, amongst several other degrees. Because closing the door on sports, opened up the one that changed his life forever and revealed his life purpose: Helping people connect with themselves and their true potential.

Johnny Martinsson is also a speaker in the field of behavioral change and how to connect with who we really are, and correct what's been dysfunctional due to previous internal programming.

Contact Johnny at: Johnnymartinsson@hotmail.com

F.A.I.L.   Faithfully Allowing IT Leverage

Live by *Design!* Not by Default

F.A.I.L.   Faithfully Allowing IT Leverage

Live by *Design!* Not by Default

F.A.I.L. Faithfully Allowing IT Leverage

Your past is not your future.

By Dr. Kim Ladson.
Life has to be more than this. I grew up in the projects of Brownsville, in Brooklyn New York. When I say this was a rough and tumble reality I still shudder thinking about it. I was born to a teenage mother who became victim to a life of drugs and all of what that entailed. I spent my early years drifting around from abandoned buildings to homelessness. That was no way for young girl to grow up. The frustration, agony, hopelessness, almost took its toll on me. I looked at my life and I knew inside that it was not for me. I wanted something different. Where I come from, I don't want anyone to ever have to go; yet the limitations of my past leveraged me to a future that I'm now proud of.

Most of the time, when we come from difficult beginnings, we get caught up in the narrative. A narrative that says that we have nowhere to go and

F.A.I.L. Faithfully Allowing IT Leverage

we are products and results of those circumstances. Circumstances many times beyond our control, yet they control us. Most of us look at those circumstances and we early on develop a language of *I can't, I don't, and I never will. I don't have the right education; I'm a failure because I failed*, we sometimes say to ourselves. We develop all the reasons why we can't, and very few reasons why we can. We look at the daunting disasters as the best hand we were dealt and accept it as our future, but it's not. Our past is not our future.

Just because our past wasn't pleasant, doesn't mean our future has to be unpleasant. My parents were caught up in the culture of the time which included drug use and lack of accountability. They were transient and often moved to less than desirable areas of town. But the whole time I lived in that environment, I always knew I wanted something different. So rather than having a pity party and inviting all my friends, I became introspective and began to write and create the future that I wanted. The bathroom became my hiding place. It was there that I would go with my black and white composition book and began to create another world for me on paper. I would write about the home I would live in, the job that I would have, the car I would drive, and the happy and blissful life that I would experience. There were no limitations, wherever my imagination would take me, I would go.

You see most of us model what we see, the circumstances around us, the situations that we face, the mentors and the role models that were given not by choice but by circumstance is what we mimic and eventually become. The greatest lesson I learned from growing up in that stark impoverished place was that I had the ability to see something different.

You see if you can look at your circumstances and know that you don't want them, know that you're

F.A.I.L.   Faithfully Allowing IT Leverage

bigger than that, know that you are better than that, you don't have to stay there. You don't have to live or relive them. Barry Kaufman said, *"The way we choose to see the world creates the world we see."* If we look at the horrible conditions and unpleasant situations that we face and focus on and dwell on that, all we do is create more of it in our future, but when we can began to see another world, a world that contradicts our circumstances, and focus on that world, then our life will began to change.

Oftentimes we look at the future and we see hopelessness, failure, and the possibility of defeat, yet that doesn't have to be the future we intend. Question...what world are you seeing? The world of your circumstances, or the world of your possibilities. Can you muster up enough strength to see the light in the midst of your darkness? The darkness of our despair oftentimes creates a future that we don't want, but we can think big in the small places. We can think Titanic, or we can think beyond the barriers that we face. We just have to allow ourselves to think. We're all born with destiny in our DNA, with public greatness and purpose.

There are times in our lives when we need an anchor to help us stay still long enough to be able to let the greatness express itself. For me, my grandmother was that anchor. My grandmother was a shining beacon of light that saw the light of Christ and shared him with me.

She would sit in a chair, look into my young eyes and say, "**you can have something different, you can be something different, you can live something different.**" I don't know why or how but I believed her. That inkling of inspiration was enough to pull me out of my desperation and give me the hope that tomorrow didn't have to be the despair I was living in.

Tomorrow could be whatever I wanted it to be and I began to craft a tomorrow that made me feel great about today. As I looked around at my squalor and my hopelessness, I knew that life had to be better. Yes, My mother fell victim to drugs, yes she was a teenager when she gave birth to me, yes, we were homeless and to some degree, hopeless, but I always saw a better future. What you look at doesn't have to be what you see, that's the new normal.

Believe God for the something better, focus on that something better, and say it if you want to see it. You can be in a circumstance or situation but that situation or circumstance doesn't have to be in you.

I'm reminded of a story of Oprah Winfrey. Her grandmother was a maid and one day she was doing laundry, she was hanging clothes on the clothing line. She stopped and looked at Oprah and said you better learn how to do this because pretty

F.A.I.L. Faithfully Allowing IT Leverage

soon that's what you going to have to do and Oprah said within herself

"*No, not me, that will not be my future."*

There are times when we, too, must look at our circumstances and say, No, not me, that will not be my future.

Oprah didn't understand it all, but somehow she knew that her life would be different than her grandmother's. Oprah's life has not been without obstacles. She was abused at a young age, she experienced many failures in her career, yet she still held on to the vision she saw for her life. As a result, Oprah Winfrey became the first African American woman to become a billionaire. Looking over her life she said, "I am where I am because of the bridges that I crossed."

The circumstances in your life are bridges. They are not final destinations, they are bridges and if you cross them, you will get to the other side. You don't have to do what you see displayed in front of you but you have to make a decision of what you want to do. Most people stay stuck in uncomfortable, unwanted, unnecessary situations because they choose to **not** choose. For me my grandmother became a catalyst for change, she nurtured me and she nurtured the dream that was within me and I followed and that dream grew into a beautiful blessing of life that I live today.

I look back on the projects and the squalor that I came from and realize that the entire time I was living it; in my mind I was living in a better future because I made the decision to not let it become a part of me. My past was not going to be my future. My grandmother taught me three very distinct and powerful lessons:

#1: Believe in God.

She taught me that believing in God would sustain me through some difficult and dangerous times. Believing in God is something that I was able to

F.A.I.L. Faithfully Allowing IT Leverage

utilize to overcome barriers and brokenness and disbelief in my life. They say in life that you are either in a problem, coming out of a problem or heading toward one. What I have found is that whichever position you find yourself in, Believing in God will always bring you through it.

#2 Believe in Yourself

You see most people don't really trust and believe in themselves. Lack of Self-belief is the beginning of most self-destruction. She taught me that in order to be able to get out of this situation that I had to *#1* believe in God but more importantly believe in myself. To believe in myself meant that I was somebody, I was worthy, and I was capable and that belief sustained me. When the reality shows different, the facts show different. We get so caught up in facts, but the facts aren't necessarily the truth, they are just a reality that we perceive to be. Charles Swindoll said that life is 10% of what happens to us, and 90% of how we react to it. It's all perception. You can do anything!

#3 Love People

The last thing she taught me and probably most important because it brought me before prominent people, is to love people in spite of the starkness of what I was going through. She taught me that by loving people it would lift me out and lift me up. I've learned to find the best in the worst, and overlook the worst in the best. My love of people has opened doors that I didn't even know were there, and closed some that could've destroyed me had I went through them.

So the question that was asked of me is how can I love others that were doing better than me? As I was in my sorrow, as I was in my shame, how can I love them that were doing better, living, eating better, living in that nice home, wearing nice clothes, when I was like Cinderella? And just as my grandmother taught me I learned those lessons well. It's easy to love someone when you love yourself. The key is not allowing the circumstances to shape you and by doing so you are able to shape the circumstances.

I learned to be happy for others. I learned that belief in that trust allowed me to apologize for circumstances beyond my control and not get caught up in wallowing in the devastation of them. As I existed in that drudgery called the Projects, the biggest project I faced was how to reconcile my love for a mother that would allow me to be in that and a grandmother who wanted to pull me out. What I love most about my mother other than the fact that she gave me life; is that she loved me, but she showed that love in different ways.

Having been caught up in the negatives of life herself, she wasn't able to give me any better than she was able to see her own self at. Drugs, abusive situations and economic dysfunction caused her to

F.A.I.L. Faithfully Allowing IT Leverage

put me in peril. Yet I learned from that lesson what I never wanted to have.

Her life choices gave me resolve that I would never allow myself to be controlled by drugs, alcohol, abuse of people, or circumstances and situations that were not pleasing to me or my situation.

I wanted to live, I wanted to live, I wanted to live well, and I wanted to live better. So I focused on that. My grandmother even though she wasn't economically better off, she was rich in love, in wisdom, and in the power of God. She always provided clean clothes and food on the table. She taught me result, she taught me respect, she taught me reality. As I live life I learned the lessons that life taught. Those lessons were many I'd like to share 3 with you right now.

#1: *You can come out different than you went in.*

F.A.I.L. Faithfully Allowing IT Leverage

If you were put into a situation that was less than wonderful you don't have to come out less than wonderful, you can come out better. You can come out different than when you went in. you don't have to conform to the shape that you were put into. The purpose of the pain and problems is to teach you and instruct how to grow and flow in life. Everyone faces obstacles in life. Your goal is to Grow and gain insight and inspiration..

#2. *There is always a lesson to be learned.*

Learn the lesson and learn it well, then share that with others. Many of us get so caught up sometimes in the living of the lesson that we don't learn from the lesson and that leaves us challenged, that leaves us in lack; that leaves us leveraged in a negative way.

#3. *Teach and share that lesson with others.*

What you learn you have to share with others to come out of it different. You always have a lesson to learn and your challenge is to teach that lesson so that others don't have to go through the struggle that you did.

Struggling isn't all-bad, sometimes struggle teaches us how to live better, how to be better, how to become better. Just like the butterfly struggled to come out of the cocoon, sometimes we have to struggle to come out of our difficult situations. Learn by growing and become better because of it.

Often we see negative environments, circumstances, and situations, when we come out of the small dark lonely place. The biggest lesson we can learn out of life is that we can think big in a small place. Begin to dream of better, hope for better, to aspire for better and better becomes your reality. We have to become a person worthy of the dreams that we dream. In order to be able to sustain a dream we have to become the person that owns that dream. Ownership requires responsibility and becomes your qualifications. All

F.A.I.L. Faithfully Allowing IT Leverage

of us find ourselves in small places every day even as adults. Sometimes you get fired; sometimes we lose a home or job, or opportunities, mates, friends. These are all small places.

To think big in those small places, regardless of the firing, the loss, or the struggle, we can think bigger and see ourselves better.

Facts are not necessarily truths; the fact is the relationship maybe over. The truth maybe you didn't need to be in a relationship in the first place.

The fact is you may have been fired from a job. The truth is God may have a better job waiting for you and need to get you out of that one in order to place you in the Better one.

We get so caught up in facts sometimes we don't understand or look at or realize the truth. We have to get beyond the facts; you have to accept the fact for truth to come a part of you. If we don't accept defeat it will not become a failure, if we don't

F.A.I.L. Faithfully Allowing IT Leverage

accept loss we're not a loser. Acceptance of the fact makes it a reality and truth. Denial is not always a river in Egypt.

You have to get to a point where you're not even concerned about the facts. Facts are going happen, but they don't have to happen to shape your reality.

I've learned to discuss what I call *my true*. You see what's true for you may just be a fact for me and I may not accept it as true. It may be reality, you may be focused on it and see it, but I don't have to accept it as *my true*. *My true* is all things work together for my good not for my despair. Facts are temporary *my true* is the only permanent, *my true* is that all things work together for the good, that I been called according to his purpose.

My true is I'm above not beneath. *My true* is I'm a winner and not a loser. *My true* is I'm a lender not a borrower. *My true* is what I accept it to be. God is everything and when you realize that he is the

F.A.I.L. Faithfully Allowing IT Leverage

essence of what makes you truly better. When you search him as I did and you'll find him as I did. Today I might be hurting, tomorrow can be a suddenly season that changes that hurt into true happiness and help.

Your past is not your future

Part of what began to take me to another place was my grandmother taking me to church. I began to breathe again, have hope and believe in a future that I could look forward to. I was born to win. And I wanted to do just that. You know there are losers and winners and then there are those people who haven't discovered how to win yet. You get to make that choice... are you going to be a loser, or will you be a winner? Or are you one of those who just haven't figured how to win yet?

Keep playing this game called life. It can make you the winner you were born to be. Even though you're struggling, God uses people to bring you salvation; God uses people to bring you strength. God uses people to bring you the stuff you need to succeed. I survived all of that and more. I went through brokenness, I went through barriers and I came out blessed. You see we all get to live through difficulties. Life is not over because we're going through a situation that has us overwhelmed.

In order to survive the struggle it is paramount that we discover the uniqueness of our **IT**. What is the **IT**?

IT is the Incredible Transformation from what is to what can be, should be, will be, and ought to be. Your **IT** is what makes you, you. But the **IT** sometimes is what we go through in the process to trying to get to. **IT** may be the circumstance, the failure, the loss, or the lack. **IT** may be the relationship that went sour, **IT** may be any number of things that cause you to come to a crucible of life and make a choice.

F.A.I.L. Faithfully Allowing IT Leverage

In this book we talk about Finally Allowing **IT** Leverage. Allowing the thing that you thought was going to destroy you to lift to back up and bring you blessing. The difference between your **IT** and your **Why** is whether you allow it to help you or to hurt you or to heal you. At the heart of the issue is whether to make you happy or to keep you in that horrible state.

It's all about your story. Everyone's story is unique and different. My mother missed the **IT** that could've leveraged her life to greatness instead she chose to live in despair. Instead I chose to see something greater, something bigger and I began to utilize my talents and my gifts to create an experience of something far greater than anything my mother knew.

That life destroyed and killed my mother, yet that same life gave me life, gave me leverage and taught me a lesson. That lesson was that God gives gifts and that we all have one and many of us have more. The key is what you do with that gift. Gifts are tied to our talents, talents are learned experiences, and gifts are examples of God-given abilities.

But if we don't use our talents and gifts we can get left behind. You have to **GET IT**. We just talked about what **IT** was. But **GET** is an acronym that means our **G**ifts **E**xperiences **T**alents. You see we can have gifts and we can have talents but if we don't utilize them and experience them, they do us little good.

Discovery of gifts leads to your life's purpose

If you're trying to figure out what's your gift, what's your talent or if what you have is a gift, look at how people perceive it. The authenticated are blessed by today, smile because of it, those are clues that you just might be operating within that God-given gift.

F.A.I.L. Faithfully Allowing IT Leverage

Our story is wrapped up in our gift, our story is what we take and share that gift with so that the people that respond to it are blessed by it. Our story is what makes us unique and when we deliver our uniqueness, we will meet with success.

Success at your gift is a talent, but you must build on it. Build on the talent and it will bring you out of those difficult situations and place you in a position of prominence, power, profit and passion.

That brought me to a turning point. As an adult I was ready to take the leap. The Leap beyond my limitations into a limitless future. After working more than 15 years in law-enforcement and a job I was not passionate about, I took the leap.

I leaped into a better life, past the 9-to-5 scheduled life to a fulfilled future that became my calling. We all have a calling. It's like expectancy or expecting a baby. You know the three phases of pregnancy don't you? If not let me share them with

F.A.I.L.   Faithfully Allowing IT Leverage

you so you can get a clearer understanding of this fundamental concept. They are simple and yet profound. The 3 phases are:

#1 **Discovery** of a life growing within you

#2 **Development** of that life

#3 **Delivery** of that life

All too often we find ourselves discovering life within, developing and never delivering it. That's unhealthy, an unfulfilled life is like having a dead fetus inside, it begins to rot and ruin our lives.

That dream within, that calling, that raison d'être is something that we have to learn to say YES to. Yesterday: yes to the greatness, yes to the possibility, yes to the impregnation within.

It's like when Mary visited Elizabeth, the child that was in Elizabeth's womb jumped because of the child that was in Mary's womb. Are you around people that make your baby leap, that make your

F.A.I.L. Faithfully Allowing IT Leverage

dream glisten and gleam, want to break free. These are the questions that have to be asked reading this book. May be the blessing is to make your baby leap, to make your baby jump on the inside, to make your dream once again become a reality.

There are ten things that I want to share with you that will help you to build your dream to think big and to make your dreams become reality.

#1. Change your environment

The first thing that I had to do in order to get out of Brownsville was to change my environment. I began to change what I reading, what I was seeing, what I was listening to, and who I was hanging around me. Jim Rohn said that we are the average of the five people we spend the most time with. Who are the five people in your life? What do they have you doing? Where do they have you going? What do they have you listening to? The ultimate question: Can the environment that you are in now, help you get to the next level? If the answer is no, It's time for a change. Don't be afraid to change your environment of your friends, your jobs, your neighborhoods, or your practices. Whatever does not add to you, will take away from you.

#2. Consistency

Master the art of everyday. We all get 24 hours in a day and it is what you do today that determines your tomorrow. Do something daily that helps to grow and develop your dream. Read a book, work on self-help. Come out of it, the baby grows in proportion to the amount of growth or the amount that you grow.

#3. Challenging self

In order to leverage your IT and go to the next level of your life, you have to challenge yourself, by doing something you never did so that you can become someone you never were. My mentor Les Brown said, we don't get in life what we want, we get in life who we are. So to get change, we must be changed, that requires that we invest in ourselves and in our growth. This challenge may require that you invest in coaches, mentors, seminars, books, and things that will add to your development.

#4. Craft Mastery

Get control of yourself. Master yourself, your gifts, your talents, your abilities, and your skills. This means you have to study, you have to practice, you have to work; you have to become competent. Tyler Cowen wrote a book called, *Average is Over."* We have to go beyond average and if you want to be great, you have to go beyond good. Mastery makes you a better person, brings you before people that can elevate you to an even higher level.

#5. *Connect to your why.*

Your why is what makes everything happen. Not sure what your why is? Your why is why you wake up and why you sleep peacefully at night. Your why is What's pulling at You!

#6. **Create value to others.**

Adding value to other people is what brings value to you. Zig Ziglar said if you help enough other people get what they want you will automatically get what you want. Look and see exactly how much value you are adding to the situation and that will determine how much value people add into your life.

#7. **Consider the power of now.**

Most people get so caught up in tomorrow or so caught up in to yesterday that they miss out on the most important time of all, which is now. If you want to get out of the circumstances, if you want to change the situation, if you want to grow, if you want to build it big, you have to do it now. Tomorrow is not promised and yesterday is something that you're not happy with because you want to change it. Make a choice to do it now. Life will challenge you, life will knock you down and when you get back up, knock you back down, but you have to resolve in your mind that you will keep getting up.

#8. Choose what you allow.

Stop allowing negativity and small minded thinking to hold you back. This will take you from significant success to significance. You see success is like happiness, it is external. Significance is like joy it's on the inside. Success is what you do, significance is what you become.

How do you make people feel that's what significance is. Adding value to your life changes

F.A.I.L. Faithfully Allowing IT Leverage

directly into the apportionment of the amount of value that you bring into other people's lives.

#9. Commit to the process of the struggle

So many people get caught up and not wanting to struggle and they wonder why they are so weak. Struggle gives you strength. It is like exercise. It builds the muscles of your mind and body. The struggle is not over until you gain the strength to win. Frederick Douglass said without struggle, there can be no progress. It is not design to break you but to make you.

#10 Count it all joy

If the odds are 1 in 1 million then you be that 1. If I could talk to young girls in school or in difficult situations in pregnancy centers and projects and ghettos across the country, I would say that if the odds are one in 1 million consider yourself, that one. That should be another truth and you get to tap into that truth, the reality isn't the truth, the

F.A.I.L.   Faithfully Allowing IT Leverage

reality is just the facts that you're dealing with. The truth is within you, and that truth is greatness. Within you there is a giant, there is a winner, there is a warrior that is waiting to win.

Bet on yourself. Life can be rough but take a chance believing in you. I did, and found something greater in me. I saw something bigger and better than the situation I was facing. I didn't allow the situation to drown me or to hold me back or prevent me from being able to step up into my greatness and help other people. To share with other people, instead I reached out and made a decision that my vision was better than my circumstance. We may have failed but we are not failures. There is something greater and that greater is waiting to express it. Your past does not have to be your future. It's called the past for a reason...it's already happened. Your future is awaiting and you can work on it right now.

Welcome to your NOW!

F.A.I.L. Faithfully Allowing IT Leverage

Bio Of Dr. Kim Ladson

Kim Ladson is one of the most dynamic Personal Development Trainers of our time. She is a dynamic personality and a highly sought after Motivator & Speaker. She serves as one of John Maxwell's Certified Leadership Trainer and Coach as well as one of Les Brown's Platinum Speakers. She has a proven record of helping others achieve their best. She is charismatic, humorous and transformational. She teaches people how to go beyond their limitations and step into their unlimited possibilities. She has helped people from all walks of life harness their potential and reach a level of great success. She has also assisted organizations in achieving high performance by providing winning formulas and practical transformational strategies.

Kim is also the author of Pulling The Best Out of You, which is a phenomenal transformational book that gives you the strategies you need to design your own life and to live a life of your dreams.

Kim has been able to achieve phenomenal success in her life by continually daring to follow her dreams. Kim has dedicated her life to the development and enhancement of people all around the world. Her dream now is to help others live their dreams and walk in their purpose and destiny. Her passion is bring the best out of others and helping them reach their greatest potential. She is the voice that helps others find their voice, and a hand that pushes others to live their best life.

Contact Kim at: Kimladson@aol.com

F.A.I.L. Faithfully Allowing IT Leverage

Live by *Design!* Not by Default

Live by *Design!* Not by Default

F.A.I.L. Faithfully Allowing IT Leverage

Why Weight to Win

By Lonnie Ford.

The average overweight person has heard so much from weight loss trainers who have never been in there shoes, doctors who never been obese, and diet pills that doesn't produce results from the so called experts. Even though I'm hundreds of pounds away from my target weight I also know that there are a lot of people struggling to just lose 5 or 10lbs, So in no way do I ignore or minimize the hardships that people that need to just lose 5 or 10 pounds because it's a hard thing to do especially when being miss informed.

I was fortunate to get into a word-based church and this put me on the true path to helping me renew my mind and because of this my body began to line up as well. I learned that distraction equals subtraction. When your distracted with life issues such as money, time, and relationships these

F.A.I.L. Faithfully Allowing IT Leverage

things will subtracted from your life mindset. See what you focus on will come upon you. There's a process to progress and gaining the right process and knowledge is crucial to making that true change. It's a daily grind of making small changes that will ultimately make the big impact, and if you're not going toward what you want you'll never get it. You have to have your mind in alignment first.

A lot of people get on fire to lose weight and fall off within 30days because they haven't aligned themselves for the journey. Less than 10% of people who makes a New Year resolution actually completes the goal they set out to do.

Why do so many people desire something with their heart and makes decisions to move toward their goal but never make it? It's because they haven't aligned there mind. You can buy a brand new set of tires for your car and put them on and if

F.A.I.L.   Faithfully Allowing IT Leverage

you don't get an alignment and balance you will need new tires next month.

An alignment changes the angle the tire meets the road. Without it you're going to have a rough ride, and you still have to have a balance with it. This is how one should approach weight-loss as well. A lot of people try to change everything that's wrong with them within a week and wonder why they can't sustain success.

You can't correct years of eating the wrong way overnight. You didn't put the weight on overnight so don't expect to take it off like that, but the good news is you can take it off. See when you begin to understand the process it will propel you, but if you don't understand the process it will paralyze you.

I found myself on a yo-yo diet going up and down, trying different pills and plans but never making true progress. You can have motivation and

F.A.I.L. Faithfully Allowing IT Leverage

aspiration but without the right education it will lead you to another dead end. See my education started like most people, at home. See when you're a kid all you know is what momma, daddy, uncle or auntie tells you. I've never met a kid who didn't eat something there mother didn't tell them to eat. I've seen mother's feed babies bottles of milk that they coughed up but eventually by force the baby will drink that formula, and grow up eating the same thing their parents eat.

Environment plays a crucial role in how successful you can become. It can decide where you start but it doesn't have to decide where you finished. Bill Gates says it like this "Starting poor is not your fought, but staying poor is". Grandma did the best she could with what she had. She taught me the best she could with what she knew, but bad information weather told to you by someone you love or someone who hates you, or someone who just doesn't understand will still do the same damage. You have to get the right information.

See I'm one who believes the word of God and it says **"Faith Comes By Hearing"** which brings me to my next point. What are you hearing? See what you hear has a great affect on what you do. Marketing specialists and big companies understands this as it relates to their business. Coco-Cola is the #1 soft drink company in the world but yet they advertise every day. No one sells more burgers than McDonald's but yet they advertise every day. Why? Because they know the more you hear them and see them the more likely you are to buy their products. They call this branding.

You've been branded by what you have chosen to listen too or what you've been forced to listen too. When I found myself in a dark and despair place where destruction was headed my way, it was the word of God that elevated my mind and propelled

F.A.I.L. Faithfully Allowing IT Leverage

me to a more progressive state of thinking . A lot of people limit their success because they are waiting on the right timing, finances, and ideal situations. I say to you Why wait to win?

My new mantra is Lose Weight And Gain Life. Lose not only the weight but the negative thoughts, the negative activities, and the negative things that causes you to gain weight in the first place. I've always been a big guy, but I did not realize how big I had become. I went a long time without weighing myself because I weighed well over 400 pounds.

A little known fact is that most scales don't go too far beyond that point. So you have to find a special spot in order to get weighed at if you way more than 400 pounds. It had been a long time since I weighed myself and I went over my friend house who was going to have surgery to help him lose weight. I asked him how much did he weigh and he said 628lbs. I asked him How did he weigh

F.A.I.L. Faithfully Allowing IT Leverage

himself and he told me he bought a special scale. When I got on the scale, I weighed in at 672 pounds. I was 28 pounds away from being 700 pounds. This was my wake-up call.

I decided from that point on I will start eating right and I was going to lose weight. So instead of eating a massive breakfast I decided just to eat cereal and bananas in the morning and cut back on some other foods I was eating. After a month I couldn't wait to weigh myself. When I jumped on the scale I was shocked that I didn't lose hardly any weight!

When I was at 350lbs going on 400lbs I said I wasn't going to get to 500lbs. When I was 500lbs I said I wasn't going to get to 600lbs and now at 672lbs I'm 28lbs from away from being 700lbs. Now that was disaster waiting to happen. I knew I couldn't continue living this way another 10yrs.

F.A.I.L. Faithfully Allowing IT Leverage

The interesting thing is that I was a very active individual for my size and had been all my life. I was able to move and I wasn't bedridden like a lot of heavy overweight individuals my size, In fact when I went to the doctor he was amazed that my blood pressure was in-line as well as my sugar level at the time. As a kid growing up my grandmother would cook the most delicious meals probably like most of the grandmothers out there. I still haven't ran across anyone who doesn't love their grandparents cooking.

I remember eating buttermilk cornbread, homemade biscuits, cakes, and more. Grandma would have two meats and three or four veggies to choose from at dinner time. She was an excellent cook and food became my drug of choice. See my mind had been getting pounded since I was a child. I was now 32 years old when I found myself getting on the scales and weighing in at 672 pounds.

F.A.I.L. Faithfully Allowing IT Leverage

When I decided to start researching and finding out what the whole process of weight loss and weight gain is all about I decided to write a book. My upcoming book is entitled "Weight Loss Advice From The 500 Guy". I choose this title because it was when I hit into the 500's I decided to write the book to help other overweight people.

You really don't have to tell an overweight person they need to lose weight. I've been told that many times as if I didn't already know I was obese. If I would go to the doctor about an ear problem they would say "You know you're overweight". I don't have enough room in this chapter to get into everything it takes to lose weight but I will get into the most important thing and that's aligning your mind for the journey.

If you truly want to lose weight you're going to have to come out head first. The main reason I went so long without having success in losing weight is because I only wanted to lose weight but

F.A.I.L. Faithfully Allowing IT Leverage

I didn't focus on it. You got to do more than want it you have to become laser focused on it. I felt like once my finances was ok I would then focus on losing weight. I felt like once I had enough time then I would go to the gym. I felt like I had a lot of other issues bigger than losing weight, and if I took care of those issues then I could focus on the weight loss.

I procrastinated around not taking care of my weight issue and when you don't take care of your issues, your issues will take care of you. When I stepped on the scale and saw I was 28 pounds from being 700lbs the first question I asked myself was WHY? Why did I let myself go so long? Why didn't I focus on this sooner? Why did I Wait To Win my Weight Battle?

The is the question I know ask others. It doesn't just apply to weight loss but to every arena in life. Why Wait To When? Waiting is the thing holding us hostage. Waiting is what preventing us from moving forward to reaching the goal of the dreams and success we have deep down in our spirits and in our minds. Yeah I was big and always knew it but I was always chasing down other things and I came to the realization that if you don't focus on what you want you want get it.

Fortunately for me I found myself in a word based church and this begin to renew my mind. It takes the right knowledge and the right information for you to be able to make a decision that can change your life. The best decision I made was start listening to positive messages. There was a lot of negative messages going on in my mind on top of dealing with negative people and having negative issues of my own.

The Most important key is that you got to get your mindset in alignment to be have success in your journey. It's what you choose to listen to that will determine what you will eventually speak and do. If you change your mindset than everything else

F.A.I.L. Faithfully Allowing IT Leverage

gets set in motion for success. You have a lot of things competing for your mind every day. You have social media, friends, co-workers, radio, television, billboards, family and much more. How much time are you dedicating to hearing positive things that will propel you into the things that you desire.

It all begins with the saturation of the right information because the wrong information can lead you down a destructive path and kill you. If you can control yourself from the neck up then from the neck down will fall in place. It's what's going in your ears that will determine what goes in your mouth and what comes out your mouth. That's why the fast food industry spends billions of dollars each year. As their dollar menu increases so does obesity and diseases. That's why pharmaceutical company's spend more on advertising then they do on medical research. If

F.A.I.L. Faithfully Allowing IT Leverage

your mind constantly get pounded with the wrong information you will never make the right choices.

From an early age I was fed a daily diet of improper food and improper information regarding food. I was not around the best eating environment. I was literally living to eat and eating to live.

Hosea Chapter 4:6 says *"my people perish because of a lack of knowledge"*.

The information that you get and listen to will either propel you or paralyze you. So I don't want to leave you without giving you a few concrete things dealing with changing your mindset.

1. ***Keep your mind open to opportunity.*** Sort of like a business you always got to keep innovating, keep your mind open to opportunity to the next thing that can take your business to the next level. Well just like that treat your body in life like a business. Make it your business to get not only your body into shape but your life into shape. To do this you got to align your mind and keep it open to opportunity.

F.A.I.L. Faithfully Allowing IT Leverage

Due to the many failures and the trying of products that don't work many people have stopped actively looking for the opportunity to lose weight. A lot of people have settled into a body and life they don't want and have put losing weight on the back end of their agendas to do. People who say I'm going to do it later, I'm too busy right now with my job, or I'm waiting to see if I'm approved for surgery, always end up a year or two down the road still in the same position. I encourage you to see the opportunity within you and your everyday life and make the decision to get the desires of your heart weather it's weight loss, starting that business, or graduating from school. *Don't Wait To Win*. It begins now with your choice. After getting this information ultimately it will still be up to you to do it.

2. ***Stay Focused. What You Focus On Will Come Upon You***! Stay Focused on your goal and at all times keep moving forward. Slow progress is better than no progress but the key is to keep moving forward with focus and consistence. Control what goes in your ears because this is what will determine

your future. Everything on earth is meant to grow weather it's an animal, a plant, or our bodies. As a child you were meant to be held for a period of time, to crawl for a period of time, and to walk for a period of time.

If your reading this book now is the time for you to run. We were meant to stretch and grow and push ourselves toward our dreams and destinies. Eagles learn to fly once there mother pushes them out the nest at an appointed time. I know for a fact that some of you reading this right now are ready to fly and all you need is a push. Get some pushers in your life.

3. **Don't Give Up.** Don't give up on becoming a healthier you. Persistence will bring you to your goal. Up's and downs will happen in your journey but don't give up even if you slip up. Encourage yourself every day into performing better than yesterday. Visualize yourself with the body and the future you are aiming so badly for and choose to live there no matter what's happening around you. Find an old picture of your desired weight and begin moving toward it. Don't let the pain paralyze you continue to your journey no matter what road blocks you many encounter. I

F.A.I.L.   Faithfully Allowing IT Leverage

promise you that your problem will go away if you can outlast the pain. Align your mind right now to know that pain is a part of the process and make the decision right now that you're going to outlast it. A lot of times it's not the situation that causes people to give up, but it's how they perceive and look at the situation. Don't listen to any voice that tells you to give up. You have to stay obsessed with success to succeed. Begin to look at and see the positive in every bad situation so that you can keep your joy in your journey.

F.A.I.L. Faithfully Allowing IT Leverage

Bio of Lonnie Ford

Lonnie Ford is a native Memphian who has struggled with obesity since childhood. As a child and adult, he has experienced the devastating physical, emotional, and financial impact of being obese. The seriousness of his situation struck him profoundly when he stepped on the scale and realized he weighed in at 672lbs.

Knowing he needed to make a drastic change he began researching weight loss strategies extensively and documenting his own journey. With tremendous support from his wife who married him at his peak weight for the man he was on the inside and drawing deeply on his faith in God, he has developed a strategy for weight loss as well as life that works!

Today, Lonnie is an encourager and exhorter of others facing the same challenges. He has a passion and purpose for seeing the potential in others and loves helping them overcome life's obstacles. Sharing his weight loss success from the perspective of someone who truly understands the cost as well as the highs and lows of being overweight, Lonnie now empowers individuals with knowledge to help them understand the dynamics of changing their mindset so that they can Lose Weight & Gain Life. In addition to motivating, encouraging, and providing solutions to others Lonnie enjoys working in his community through his church.. He's further encouraged by Jeremiah 29:11 which says, *"For I know the plans I have for you declares the Lord, plans to prosper you and not to harm you, plans to give you hope and a future"* and Mark 9:23 *"If thou can believe, all things are possible to him that believeth"*.

2020lonnieford@gmail.com

F.A.I.L.   Faithfully Allowing IT Leverage

Live by *Design*
Not by Default

F.A.I.L. Faithfully Allowing IT Leverage

Learn to enjoy life's Golden Moments.

By Adrian Starks

When gold goes through fire all the dross and impurities are burned out. What is left is pure gold and it is more valuable than what went into the fire. The gold is now golden and polished. The smelter now says that you can see your reflection clearly in the liquid, it's pure. One of the things that mar our reflection is the dross they see when people look within us.

We carry the weights of past failures and other problems that are your reflection. The test of time is when we are in the fire and that fire is designed to refine us, define us but not confine us. When we go through that test the final result is that we're done, we are finished and part of us has diminished. It gives way to the fire in you and the pain that follows only leads to a bigger and much greater gain.

When we are faced with fear, we have two choices, Face Everything And Rise or Forget Everything And Run. All too often we choose the latter course. IF we faced everything and rose above the things that we thought were there to destroy us, we could see that those very things would become the things that actually deliver us. What we are confronting and what is facing us is there so that we can find ourselves, find the courage and discover our strength. When faced with challenges IF we forget everything and run we will never learn the lesson. Each of us are required to learn new lessons every day and those lessons can sometimes be painful. The purpose of the pain like the fire is to refine us. Those unwilling to face the pain will have to face it again and again until it is enough to cause us to not be victims of repeated mistakes or failures.

F.A.I.L.   Faithfully Allowing IT Leverage

I experienced this lesson through one of my own personal fire sand personal flames. I once loved and committed myself to a loving relationship and my mate walked away. This was one of the most painful experiences of my life. I was in that fire and the relentless burning temperature had no care for the penetrating pain.

Facing a painful moment is what will get you beyond that moment. Most people are unwilling to face the thing that is bringing the greatest pain, but in the end if you courageously stay in to win it, can bring the greatest breath of reward and the most joy. Like gold it burns away all the awful impurities with a new polished feel and frees you of the dross. The dross is what causes people to see us and think it would not be complete and that we would not finish our process. The pain in the fire burns off, removes, eviscerates and allows us to come out shining like pure gold and those are the golden moments that life is all about.

F.A.I.L. Faithfully Allowing IT Leverage

Failure is necessary to win, to succeed, to learn, and to grow. Without failure the systems in place are false, so we have to fail our way to success. It was formula 409 which meant that there were 408 failures, there were 39 failures before WD40, Heinz 57 sauce had 56 other recipes that didn't work. The point is failure is the path of success. He who is unwilling to fail is unable to win, that's what success is all about, going through that incredible process and being willing and able to endure.

My whole life I had been looking for answers for self-validation through people and I failed myself, I failed everyone else, but the end result is that the failures led to the success in finding myself. In finding myself, I discovered who I was and what value I had to others. Difficulty is needed to develop destiny. The easy road only leads to ruin.

F.A.I.L. Faithfully Allowing IT Leverage

It's necessary to embrace the pain, or it will embrace you. It will cause you to end up not as a butterfly that Maya Angelou describes in her poem but as someone that keeps falling into the fire. Escaping the pain prevents the game from being fully played out. Just as the butterfly was able to fly away from a dark and dreary situation of its cocoon, we have to have the opportunity at the struggle from pain and flame within to be able to become more and to rise and fly from our darkness and dreariness.

Circumstances don't create us but reveal us. Our truth is that which is true about us, that which is real about us, that which is not just fact but is centered on reality, authenticity and significance.

Loving anything or anyone is a risk we all take. With this risk there comes the possibility of a setback, disappointment or even a loss. This is all

F.A.I.L. Faithfully Allowing IT Leverage

part of the process of the fire to make us learn and grow to become stronger. I'm not saying that if something distasteful happens to us that we should smile because we deserve it. No, I am saying that life will happen and we can't predict what happens to us or around us. What really counts is what happens inside of us. So, what is your internal dialogue within yourself that can help you to not only survive but thrive.

I use to feel that if I lived life just going along to get along, a lot of good things should happen. But should and did are two different things. People should open doors, people should be nice to people, people should pay the tithes, people should pay their bills but all too often they don't do any of the things they should. And when those people don't do what they should, they end up following instead of leading their authentic self. They find themselves blindly following when they could

F.A.I.L.   Faithfully Allowing IT Leverage

have instead been leading themselves to the point of achieving what they want to be.

What do you want to be? I want you to take time right now and write three things that you truly desire and act as if money time or ability play no factor in it.

1. _____

_____

_____

2. _____

_____

_____

3. _____

_____

_____

I spent so many years in my cocoon like the caterpillar putting my life on hold not trying to fly like the butterfly. Fear of failing did that to me and I allowed it. Don't do the same. There will never be a perfect time to love yourself unconditionally and start living the life you were destined to live. Never be afraid to ask for help. There are times when you will be unwilling to go to your family and friends because of judgment. Realize that by not getting help you are judging yourself. Get advice from someone who you trust or look up to as a way of starting to find some answers to the questions in your life. I was faced with the daunting task in my world, but around me I called one person that I felt comfortable with. The one person that I thought that I could confide in and tell my deepest feelings to was my younger brother. As I trembled in regret of not believing in myself he looked at me and with a supportive look on his face and told me a new story that I hadn't even heard before...**he looked up to ME!**

"You can't give up on yourself! Your dreams are stronger than that and you are much stronger than the situations that bring challenges. I need you to

F.A.I.L. Faithfully Allowing IT Leverage

stay strong because you are my superhero" and I stopped. "I'm your superhero" I asked?

" Yes, you've always been my superhero, you've always been the person that I looked up to. You know you support everyone around you and everyone is depending on you so you can't quit you can't give up, you got to learn to save yourself. You always try to save everybody else. Now it is time to take your own advice. Learn to save yourself and the person that you need to save is you. You have to change your train of thoughts."

"You have to stop the blame game, stop blaming yourself, stop blaming others. Say yes to forgive and move on. Yes, to release the anger, the fear, release the baggage and dadgummit you got to step up and step out, and get out of step, step in and save yourself."

F.A.I.L. Faithfully Allowing IT Leverage

I looked at him and he looked to me and said "I always listen to you but now listen to me. There is someone that has helped me weather some storms in my life. Have you ever heard of Les Brown"?I admitted I had not.

"You've never heard of Les Brown and you are supposed to be Mr. Inspiration Adrian? He chuckled. Look him up, go to YouTube and listen to some of Les Brown's motivational videos and get back to me. I'm surprised YOU have never heard of Les Brown!"

Now I was intrigued, I had to find out who this LES BROWN was. Well I did listen to Les Brown **all night** and when I finished listening to all of his material I said that's what I want to do, I want to do exactly what Les Brown is doing. I want to motivate and inspire and encourage people. The most important thing I learned that night was when Les Brown said *"when life knocks you down at least*

F.A.I.L. Faithfully Allowing IT Leverage

land on your back because if you can look up you can get up" and I've been getting up ever since.

Stop having a pity party and you are the only person attending. That was a defining moment for me that made a big difference in my life. I realized it was time for me to retrain my brain. I learned it was time for me to be **selfish**. Now we've been taught all of our life not to be selfish and always look out for other people and that's important, but it's just as important or maybe more so to look out for yourself.

That's not necessarily selfish, that's being self-focused. Train your brain and learn to study and have something positive to input into your mind, into your brain anytime, anywhere, all the time, everywhere.

You know we have so much negative input all day long. Eight hours of work, often all negative input.

F.A.I.L.   Faithfully Allowing IT Leverage

Then the television, so many hours of video games, so many hours of so much content, most of it negative and we wonder why we end up with a negative outlook on life. You need to start listening to positive input so that you can become safe, healed and satisfied.

What we see, we become, what we think about becomes our reality. If what you're thinking about is any indication of what you're listening to, reading, looking at, feeling, being exposed to, there is no wonder most lives are so off course and off centered.

The golden moments are what we all need to look for, they are what our life is all about. I wondered why I was surrounded with so many negative outcomes. Then I began to realize that I was attracting them. I was attracted to them and the reason that I was continuously attracting uncommitted people and situations was because I

F.A.I.L. Faithfully Allowing IT Leverage

wasn't committed to myself. Expect to be treated successful and you will be. Expect to be treated with respect and you will be respected or learn to go around the things in life that give you your respect. You have the option, you have a chance and the choice to make a decision to go with your own vision or to follow that of someone else.

You have to have a calendar because without a calendar you have no control, without a calendar someone uses circumstances and situations to control you. You must have a written calendar of events that you're going to do daily. Take back your power. You gain control back of your own life. You can only control what you see and you can only control yourself. Oftentimes we relinquish control by not having a schedule, not having a dream, not having a written vision that we're seeking ideal cause and so we get caught up.

F.A.I.L.   Faithfully Allowing IT Leverage

However, when you reach and react properly you are able to become more valuable than gold or silver. We are all unaware of the circumstances around us and until we get awareness we will continue to fail. You shouldn't continue to be part of someone else's plan for their success and not our own.

Believe in yourself. If you don't try how are you going to reach your reward? Reaction is lack of control in the situation, response is complete control. We're all extraordinary, what separates the ordinary from the extraordinary is a little **extra**. All of us have that little extra. There are three things that we all have that make the difference for what we all want.

Those three things are:

#1: Time

Have you ever noticed that the hands of time only move forward?

F.A.I.L.   Faithfully Allowing IT Leverage

#2: A brain

We all have a mind. We can use it all week or let it be used by others. What we view, we can control, what we focus on, can be controlled. All the negative chatter in our mind can be controlled if we have dreams and written goals and directions.

#3 is we all have gifts and talents

Your job is to sharpen them, sharpen the gifts, hone the skills to razor sharpness. What you love, what you want, what you focus on is what you will see manifested in your reality.

Abraham Lincoln said that **if he had 8 hours to chop down a tree he would spend the first six hours sharpening the axe**. That's what successful people do, they prepare for situations. So start preparing and sharpening those minds. I believe in what Earl Nightingale said, "we only use 10% of our mind and if we were to use 5%-10% more we would be able to memorize the entire encyclopedia and learn

F.A.I.L. Faithfully Allowing IT Leverage

over 40 languages". Man and woman are awesome beings.

Money should serve us we shouldn't serve it. We should use our gifts to chop up the tree of success and then build a ladder so that we can reach the dreams that we have, no matter what they are. Paul Brandt would say to "**Don't tell me the sky is the limit when there are footprints on the moon.**" Failure is a privilege that you don't deserve to employ or enjoy. In Victor Frankl's epic book ***Man's Search for Meaning*** he discussed his time in a concentration camp. He found that even in despair that men had a choice and the choices were dependent on what they thought of their life or expected. What do you expect from your life and that will give you a better meaning of what you can give?

He found that if you had a defined purpose you could indeed survive any trial placed upon the human soul. Your expectation was your survival.

F.A.I.L.   Faithfully Allowing IT Leverage

Earl Nightingale would teach that we just can't expect things from life however without first giving. If you failed to put the wood in the fireplace you had no right to expect to get the heat. And that's how we are sometimes asking for something that we haven't prepared for. You can't say give me heat and if you haven't put in the proper requirements. In order to get the heat, it requires wood. Provide a service, get moving, get busy. Stop standing still if you expect better results. They only come to the man that is prepared.

One of the most fascinating facts that I found out about life is that the world spins regardless if I'm here or not. At first that was a sobering fact, then I realized it is most important realization that I ever come to.

We are required to do something. Here is my idea of success explained in a well-known scientific formula. It is this $f X d = W$ physics equation. **Force times Distance equals Worth**. That means the

F.A.I.L.   Faithfully Allowing IT Leverage

amount of Effort that you put in and the Distance you are willing to go will go determine your Worth and Value. In that you are literally putting in that extra gives you more value. Say it is my time to win, my time to succeed, my time to move forward. You can own your own lane. One of the great joys that I get is to volunteer with a group of pre-K kids once a month for story time reading. When I walk in and read to these children, there is something within me that says *"you are doing great and will be okay."* Sure I experienced some pains and so have you. You are still here to make things happen. So get to work.

Do what you love and reach beyond your comfort zones to attain your true worth like gold. You are golden. Know that your pains in life is just the emotional energy that is needed to remove your impurities. You will come out of the fire because you have a date with destiny. You have a

F.A.I.L. Faithfully Allowing IT Leverage

wonderful day, WONDERFUL life and don't forget to enjoy the golden Moments.

Bio of Adrian Starks

Adrian Starks, speaker and consultant, shares his knowledge in human development and communication services with 16 years in the health and medical field. He believes that everyone has a unique significance to the world and the goal is to help them search, believe and act upon that potential. As a personal trainer and consultant for multiple facilities, he has helped clients reach individual goals through effective means of structure, communication and awareness of one's full potential to succeed. His advanced communication skills were shared as a leading Family Services Coordinator for one of the top 10 hospitals in the country. He has reached the highest ranked title in that occupation as a top performer. Adrian is actively involved as a speaker and looks to continue to leave his legacy in the world through the power of spoken and shared words from the stage to the page.

"We must learn to plant positive seeds of thoughts that will grow the ideas to eventually blossom into successful achievements" Adrian Starks

Contact me at: adrianstarks@gmail.com

F.A.I.L.   Faithfully Allowing IT Leverage

Live by *Design!*
Not by Default

www.ingramcontent.com/pod-product-compliance
Lightning Source LLC
LaVergne TN
LVHW051606070426
835507LV00021B/2795